FOR TODAY'S

HUSTLERS

BY:

MARCUS A. SHEALEY

WITH PEOPLE BEING CREATURES OF HABIT, THE RULE OF THUMB IS IF THEY'VE DONE IT ONCE THEY'LL PROBABLY DO IT AGAIN. THAT'S A RISK U TAKE WHEN YOU FORGIVE SO CHOOSE WISELY WHEN IT COMES TO WHOM YOU CHOOSE TO CUT OFF AND WHOM YOU CHOOSE TO BE PATIENT WITH...

PEOPLE WILL PURPOSELY STEAL YOUR JOY AND
PAINT A PICTURE TO OTHERS TO FIT THE DECOR
OF THE PERCEPTION THAT THEY WANT OTHERS
TO HAVE OF THE SITUATION...

THE ILLUSION OF BEING REAL BECOMES A FADED MEMORY WHEN THE WATERMARK WASHES OFF AND ITS EXPOSED FOR BEING FAKE... AN ILLUSION WILL ONLY LAST AS LONG AS YOU BELIEVE AND ALLOW IT TO BE REAL...

KNOWING WHERE IT IS THAT YOU WANT TO END UP IS ONLY THE BEGINNING OF THE BATTLE OF GETTING THERE...

KNOWING WHERE IT IS THAT YOU WANT TO END UP IS ONLY THE BEGINNING OF THE BATTLE OF GETTING THERE...

HOW CAN YOU BLATANTLY BE DISRESPECTFUL
TO YOURSELF BUT THEN COMPLAIN ABOUT
SOMEONE ELSE DISRESPECTING YOU?

REFUSING TO LET GO OF SITUATIONS IN YOUR LIFE WILL CONTINUE TO BLOCK YOUR OWN BLESSINGS BECAUSE THOSE SAID SITUATIONS TAKE UP THE VACANT SPACES THAT YOUR BLESSINGS WOULD OTHERWISE OCCUPY... DO NOT BE THE WEAPON FORMED AGAINST YOURSELF...

WHEN YOU VISUALIZE YOUR LIFE AND THINK
ABOUT ALL YOU'VE DONE, ITS AMAZING TO SEE
JUST HOW FAR YOU'VE ACTUALLY COME.
NEVER FORGET TO TAKE THE TIME TO GIVE
YOURSELF GRACE AND TAKE IT ALL IN...

WHEN SOMEONE TRIES TO KICK YOU WHEN YOU'RE DOWN, BREAK THEIR LEG OFF, AND USE IT TO GET BACK UP... PEOPLE ARE THE MOST DISRESPECTFUL WHEN THEY FEEL AS THOUGH YOU DON'T HAVE A FIGHTING CHANCE AND HAVE LOST ALL HOPE

HOW DO YOU FORGET WHERE YOU CAME FROM IF YOU "RESPECT" WHERE YOU HAVE BEEN...

ALWAYS WATCH YOUR BACK CAUSE
EVENTHOUGH IT'S HARD TO HATE SOMEONE
WHEN THEY'RE DOING SOMETHING GOOD FOR
YOU, THERE'S STILL ALWAYS A CHANCE THAT
THE DECIETFULS' HEART IS STILL SET ON
DECIET...

HAVING THE VISION IS THE FIRST STEP AT
FULLFILLING A DREAM...

IT'S FUNNY HOW PEOPLE SO EASILY FORGET
ABOUT ALL THE SACRAFICES YOU HAVE MADE
AND THE THINGS THAT YOU HAVE DONE, ONCE
THEY DECIDE TO BETRAY AND DECIEVE YOU...

PEOPLE ARE SO "COMPASSIONATE" UNTIL ITS TIME TO SHOW SOME "COMPASSION", SO "UNDERSTANDING" TILL ITS TIME TO "UNDERSTAND", SO "EMPATHETIC" TILL ITS TIME TO SHOW SOME "EMPATHY", SO SYMPATHETIC TILL ITS TIME TO SHOW SOME "SYMPATHY", SO "CARING" TILL ITS TIME TO SHOW HOW MUCH THEY CARE... PEOPLE CAN BE SOME OF THE "MOST" UNTIL ITS TIME TO "SHOW" AND PUT ACTION BEHIND THOSE WORDS...

TO REFILL YOURSELF WITH HAPPINESS YOU
HAVE TO RELINQUISH THE PAINS OF YOUR
PAST...

EVERYONE HAS THEIR OWN PERSONAL
VERSION OF JUDAS IN THEIR LIFE, BUT EVEN HE
WAS FORGIVEN FOR HIS TREACHORY...

IT TAKES A STRONG PERSON TO FORGIVE AND
ULTIMATELY IT SHOWS YOUR HIGHEST
ELEVATION OF GROWTH, SO IT'S OK FORGIVE,
BUT NEVER FORGET...

CONTINUING TO REVISIT A WRONG ONLY
POISONS THE PERSON DOING THE REVISITING...

PEOPLE ABANDON THOSE THEY WERE USING
BECAUSE THOSE WHOM THEY TRULY LOVE
THEY HOLD IN A DIFFERENT LIGHT AND
WOULDN'T DARE JEOPARDIZE LOSING THEM...

DONT BECOME SO ENGULFED IN PROVING
YOURSELF TO SOMEONE WHOM ISN'T
INVESTED ENOUGH IN YOU TO DO THE SAME IN
RETURN...

TIME...
DOES NOT ERASE MEMORY... NOR DOES IT
REPAIR OR REPLACE THE EXPERIENCES BURIED
WITHIN IT...

A SCAR IS A SIGN THAT THE WOUND IS CLOSED
BUT IT DOESNT NECESSARILY MEAN THAT THE
HURT IS OVER NOR THAT ITS HEALED.
EVERYTHING IS A PROCESS, FOR SOME
WOUNDS INFLICT DIFFERENT TYPES OF
INFLICTIONS...

THROUGHOUT YOUR LIFETIME YOU WILL LEAVE
LITTLE PIECES OF YOUR HEART IN SO MANY
DIFFERENT PLACES THAT YOU WILL PROBABLY
BE LEFT WITH ONLY ENOUGH TO LIVE OFF OF
WITH HOPES OF FINDING SOMEONE TO
NOURISH IT, MAKE IT WHOLE, & FLOURISHING
AGAIN....

A SQUARE INSIDE OF YOUR CIRCLE WILL
ALWAYS ALTER THE WAY THAT YOU ROLL...

BEWARE OF A BLOWOUT FROM TRYING TO
KEEP SOMETHING OR SOMEONE INYOUR
CIRCLE THAT DOESN'T ULTIMATELY FIT...

IT'S CALLED PREVENTATIVE MAINTENANCE...

LET PEOPLE DO WHAT THEY WANNA DO, THAT
WAY YOU CAN SEE WHERE YOU FALL IN
REFERENCE TO THEIR LIST OF PRIORITIES...

BE CAREFUL WITH A NEW CONNECTION
BECAUSE IT CAN ULTIMATELY END UP BEING A
DISCONNECTION IN DISQUISE...

TO SATISFY AN APPETITE FOR DESTRUCTION,
YOU SOMETIMES HAVE TO PUT IT ON A
RECONSTRUCTIVE DIET...

SOMETIMES YOU HAVE TO REVISIT YOUR PAST TO RECIEVE THE FUTURE THAT YOU DESERVE....

REMEMBER THIS IS YOUR SEASON OF PREPARATION AND PREPARATION REQUIRES A THOROUGH STUDY OF THE PAST...

YOU MAY NOT GET OVER EVERYTHING THAT HAPPENS TO YOU BUT ONE WAY OR ANOTHER YOU CAN GET THROUGH IT CAUSE NOONE HAS WENT THROUGH LIFE WITH A FLAWLESS VICTORY...

BUILD OFF OF YOUR PAST TO SOLIDIFY YOUR PRESENT WHILE SECURING YOUR FUTURE, BY MAKING THE CONSCIOUS EFFORT TO FOCUS ON THE CORRECTION OF SELF AND NOT THE PERCEPTION OF SELF BECAUSE WE OFTEN OVERLOOK THE MOST IMPORTANT THINGS IN FRONT OF US...

WORK ON HEALING IT HINDERS, WORK ON
RELEASING OLD ENERGY IT MAKES YOU
COMPLACENT. YOU MUST ALIGN YOUR
PASSIONS WITH YOUR PURPOSE WITH YOUR
INTENTIONS, WHEN WORKING ON MAKING
NEW CONNECTIONS TO FILL OLD VOIDS...

SOMETIMES OUR MOST FORMIDABLE FOES USUALLY CAMOFLAUGE THEIR BIGGEST WEAKNESSESS AS THEIR GREATEST STRENGTHS...

TIME...IT'S SUCH A FUNNY THING... WHEN YOU ARE AROUND, PEOPLE CAN FIND COUNTLESS THINGS THAT THEY'D LIKE FOR YOU TO DO WITH YOUR TIME... THEY WANT YOU TO INVEST IT, SPEND IT, FIND IT, GIVE IT, TAKE IT, CREATE IT, MAKE IT, AND SOMETIMES THE MOST INCONSIDERATE OF PEOPLE EVEN WANT YOU TO WASTE IT! BUT FALL OUT OF THAT LOOP AND WATCH HOW MANY OF THOSE SAME PEOPLE EITHER CAN'T FIND, DONT HAVE, OR WON'T MAKE THAT SAME TIME FOR YOU...

WHEN IT SEEMS THAT THINGS WILL NOT TURN AROUND FOR YOU, AND ANY AND EVERYTHING THAT YOU CAN THINK OF JUST CONTINUES TO GO WRONG. SOMETIMES YOU HAVE TO LOOK AT YOUR CIRCLE, ELEVATE AND ELEVIATE YOUR MINDSET, AND SACRFIFICE SITUATIONS IN YOUR LIFE THAT YOU HAVE BEEN HOLDING ON TO THAT NO LONGER SERVE A PURPOSE...

WISDOM IS HARD TO SWALLOW...SO
TOMORROW EXPECT APOLOGIES... WHEN
BEING REAL, SOMETIMES THEY NEVER BELIEVE
YOU UNTIL THEY FIND OUT YOU KNEW EXACTLY
WHAT YOU WERE TALKING ABOUT...

EVERYTHING ISNT ALWAYS FOR EVERYONE TO KNOW, SO SAVE SOME OF YOUR BUSINESS OR YOU WILL NOT HAVE ANY FOR YOURSELF...

IT TAKES A STRONG MAN TO RECOGNIZE HIS MISTAKES AND FLAWS, AND AN EVEN STRONGER ONE TO ATTEMPT TO CORRECT THEM...

GROWTH...

HOW CAN YOU BE A PART OF THE SOLUTION IF
YOU CONTINUE TO BE AN UNDERLYING PART
OF THE PROBLEM...

LET YOUR SUCCESSES INSPIRE MORE
ACCOMPLISHMENTS WHILE ALLOWING YOUR
FAILURES TO TEACH UNFORGETTABLE LESSONS
ON HOW TO CONTINUE TO SUCCEED...

A BUSY MIND ONLY RESTS AT ITS SUCCESS AND
EVEN THEN, IT'S STILL WORKING ON ITS NEXT
SUCESSFUL MOVE...

SOMETIMES ITS SMARTER TO ACCEPT A LOSS
THAN TO CREATE A BIGGER PROBLEM
ATTEMPTING TO RECTIFY IT...

IF YOU CHANGE BUT CAN'T CHANGE THE PEOPLE AROUND YOU, THEN EVENTUALLY THE PEOPLE AROUND YOU WILL NEED TO CHANGE...

AT A CERTAIN POINT IN LIFE, YOU CAN'T LOOK
AT POTENTIAL YOU HAVE TO LOOK AT
FOUNDATION OR YOU WILL FIND YOURSELF
TRYING TO GIVE SOMEONE THE WORLD WHOS
ONLY READY FOR THE CITY...

THE WEIGHT OF THE WORLD ON YOUR SHOULDERS CAN SOMETIMES BE UNBEARABLE AND SEEMINGLY NEVER BE ALLIEVIATED UNTIL YOU SHIFT YOUR FOCUS FROM HOW HEAVY THE WEIGHT IS, TO BECOMING STRONGER TO MAKE CARRYING THAT WEIGHT EASIER...

SOMETIMES DISAPPEARING OFF THE SCENE
CAN GRANT U AN UNEXPECTED ADVANTAGE TO
TAKING A NEW APPROACH TO AN OLD
DREAM...

ITS BETTER TO REMINISCE THAN TO REGRET...
YOUR FATE HOLDS MORE WEIGHT THAN YOUR
MEMORIES....

SOMETIMES YOU HAVE TO PLACE YOURSELF IN
AN UNCOMFORTABLE SITUATION IN ORDER TO
REACH THE LEVEL OF COMFORT THAT YOU
ULTIMATELY DESIRE...

PRESENT SACRAFICES PROMOTE SUCCESSFUL
FUTURES...

WE ALL HAVE A STRANGE TENDENCY TO OVER
VALUE AND IDEALIZE OUR SIGNIFICANT
OTHER... DONT TRICK YOURSELF, BY PLACING
MORE VALUE ON THEM THEN THEY PLACE ON
THEMSELVES...

BE CONTENT WITH LOSING A BATTLE IN ORDER
TO WIN THE OVERALL WAR...

THINGS DON'T ALWAYS GO AS PLANNED, TAKE
THE "L" FOR THE BIGGER PICTURE. THEREIS
ALWAYS WINTER TO "FALL" BACK ON...

IF YOU KNOW THAT YOU AREN'T ON THE SAME PAGE AS SOMEONE ELSE, THEN WHY WOULD YOU EVEN OPEN THEIR BOOK...

YOU CAN NEVER HAVE ANYTHING AMOUNGST
THOSE THAT HAVE NOTHING UNLESS YOU PLAN
TO HAVE NOTHING AS WELL...

THE STREETS DONT LOVE YOU... THEY JUST
EVENTUALLY, IN ONE WAY OR ANOTHER, FIND
A WAY TO TAKE YOU AWAY FROM THOSE IN
YOUR LIFE THAT DO...

RULE OF THUMB... THE BEST PLACE TO BUILD A BUSINESS IS THE SAME PLACE WHERE YOU CAN FIND THE PROBLEM THAT NEEDS ATTENDING TO...

REMEMBER... THE ROLE THAT YOU WERE GIVEN IN LIFE IS NOT THE ROLE THAT YOU HAVE TO ACCEPT AND LIVE OUT BECAUSE YOUR FUTURE MIRRORS THE ACTIONS OF YOUR PAST...

BEFORE YOU START ANYTHING, LEARN HOW TO FINISH IT. SEEING THE OUTCOME THAT YOU WANT IS THE BEGINNING BECAUSE YOU ALWAYS KNOW WHERE YOU WANNA BE AT THE END...

EACH AND EVERYONE OF US HAVE SCARS FROM OUR PAST WHETHER THEY ARE PHYSICAL OR EMOTIONAL. THERE IS A CERTAIN BEAUTY TO EACH ONE OF THESE SCARS BECAUSE THEY ALL HAVE A STORY BEHIND THEM THAT HAS YET TO BE TOLD. BUT THE MOST BEAUTIFUL STORY OF THEM ALL IS THE FACT THAT, YOU ARE STILL HERE...

TRUST YOURSELF AND ALLOW THAT ENERGY
AND INTUITION TO GUIDE YOU SO THAT YOU
WILL INVEST MORE INTO WHAT YOU FEEL
RATHER THAN WHAT YOU THINK...

IF YOU CAN'T BE TRUE TO YOURSELF THEN YOU CAN'T BE TRUE TO ANYONE ELSE... YOU CAN'T REPAIR YOURSELF FROM WITHIN IF YOU ARE IN DENIAL...

STOP REWINDING THINGS THAT NEED TO BE
DELETED...

PEOPLE WILL PREDETERMINE YOUR DESTINY
WITH PUNCTUATION LIKE THAT OF A SENETNCE
BY PLACING A "PERIOD", WHICH MARKS AN
END. IN A PLACE WHERE THERE SHOULD BE A
"COMMA," SHOWING THE INTENT OF
CONTINUATION...

NEVER ALLOW ANYONE TO TELL YOUR STORY
BECAUSE THEY WILL DICTATE AN ENDING
WHERE YOU ARE STILL GOING AND GROWING...

INSTEAD OF TRYING TO TEAR OTHERS DOWN
TRY EARNING RESPECT, INCLUDING SELF
RESPECT, ITS BETTER THAN BEING A PARASITE...

WHEN YOU START TO QUESTION WHO IT IS THAT YOU'VE BECOME, LOOK AROUND AT THE PEOPLE YOU'VE HELPED AND WHAT THEY'VE BECOME, AND AT THAT POINT YOU WILL REALIZE WHETHER OR NOT YOU HAVE DONE WELL OR IF YOU STILL HAVE WORK TO DO TO BETTER YOURSELF...

ANYONE WHOM HAS SUCCEEDED HAS HAD TO
CHANGE SOMETHING... CHANGE IS INEVITABLE,
ESPECIALLY WHEN IN THE PURSUIT OF SUCCESS.
A PERSON WILLING TO CHANGE IS A PERSON
THAT'S WILLING TO DO WHAT IT TAKES TO
SUCCEED...

THE MOST IMPORTANT CHANGES IN ORDER
FOR THE NEXT SEASON OF YOUR LIFE TO BE
COMPLETE, LIES ON YOUR ABILITY TO FIND THE
GOOD IN GOODBYE...

MOST DONT HAVE ENOUGH IMAGINATION TO
DEAL WITH THEIR OWN REALITY...

SO THEY LIVE VICARIOUSLY THROUGH YOURS...

SOMETIMES WHEN YOU DO THE RIGHT THING IT DOESNT WORK OUT, BUT THAT DOESNT MEAN THAT IT WASNT WORTH DOING...

PAST ENDEAVORS CAN TARNISH THE
POSSIBILITY OF FUTURE INVESTMENTS...

HABBITS ARE LIKE CHAINS... THEY CAN HOLD YOU BACK, TIE YOU DOWN, OR RESTRICT YOUR MOVEMENT, AND YOU WILL NEVER KNOW THEIR STRENGTH UNTIL YOU ATTEMPT TO BREAK THEM...

EVENTHOUGH THERE IS ALWAYS A LIGHT AT
THE END OF THE TUNNEL, IT'S THE DARKNESS
THAT YOU HAVE TO TRAVEL THOUGH IN ORDER
TO GET THERE THAT YOU HAVE TO BE WORRIED
ABOUT. SO FOR EVERY SITUATION YOU HAVE
TO FIND THE FLASHLIGHT OF GUIDANCE
THROUGH OBTAINING THE RIGHT KNOWLEDGE
AND WISDOM TO MAKE YOUR JOURNEY
THROUGH THE DARKNESS EASIER....

OFTEN TIMES WE RESIST SEEING OURSELVES AS
HAVING FELL FOR JUST ANYONE BECAUSE IT
REFLECTS BADLY ON WHO WE ARE SINCE WE'RE
MORE LIKELY TO FALL FOR SOMEONE WHOM
MIRRORS US IN SOME WAY, SHAPE, OR FORM...

SOMETIMES YOU HAVE TO INTENTIONALLY
FALL BACK JUST TO SEE IF THEY'LL SHOW
ENOUGH INTEREST TO FALL FORWARD...

BE LEARY OF THE MESSAGES HIDDEN INSIDE OF
THE WAY THAT PEOPLE JOKE WITH YOU FOR
THEY HOLD THE TRUE MEANING OF THE WAY
THAT THEY SEE, THINK, & FEEL ABOUT YOU...

YOU CAN LEARN A LOT MORE ABOUT A PERSON
BY WATCHING THEM, THAN YOU WOULD
PROBABLY LEARN BY LISTENING TO THEM...SO
TRY LISTENING TO THEIR ACTIONS...

SOMETIMES WE NEED LOVE IN DOSES AND AT TIMES THE LOVE THAT WE ARE LOOKING FOR ISN'T THE LOVE THAT WE RECIEVE... BUT... ITS THE LOVE THAT WE NEED IN ORDER TO PREPARE US FOR THE LOVE THAT WE ULTIMATELY WANT...

NEVER SETTING A GOAL IS THE ONLY WAY THAT
YOU WILL NEVER ACHIEVE ONE...

SOMETIMES YOU HAVE TO ROLL WITH THE PRESENT, TO PRESENT THE FUTURE THAT YOUR PAST DIDNT PRODUCE...

PEOPLE HATE WHAT THEY CAN'T CONQUER, FEAR WHAT THEY DONT UNDERSTAND, ENVY WHAT THEY CAN'T HAVE, AND DESTROY MOST OF WHAT THEY ALREADY POSESS.... GREED IS MORE POWERFUL THAN YOU CAN EVER IMAGINE...

SOMETIMES IN LIFE, IN ORDER TO SLOW DOWN
YOU HAVE TO TAKE THE EXIT AND PREPARE TO
TRAVEL THE ROAD LESS TRAVELED OR YOU
WILL JUST END UP SPEEDING BACK UP AGAIN...

SHARING YOUR TRUTH CAN KEEP SOMEONE ELSE FROM HAVING TO LIVE THE SAME NIGHTMARE, AND THEFORE, SHARING THE SAME TRUTH...

THOSE WHO STUMBLE OR LOSE THEIR FOOTING
OFTEN TIMES PLANT THEIR NEXT STEP ON
MORE STURDY GROUND BY PLANNING AHEAD
BECAUSE THEY NOW KNOW WHAT TO EXPECT
FROM THE LAST TIME THEY STUMBLED...

GOD WILL PLACE A TOTAL STRANGER IN YOUR
LIFE TO GET YOU TO WHERE YOURE SUPPOSED
TO BE BECAUSE THOSE THAT YOU THOUGHT
WHERE THERE TO SUPPORT YOU THOUGHT
THAT IF THEY DIDN'T SUPPORT YOU, THEN IT
WOULD ULTIMATELY HOLD YOU BACK...

AINT NOTHING WRONG WITH BEING A GIVER
BUT SOMETIMES THE GIVER NEEDS HELP TOO!
AND THE TAKERS HAVE NO UNDERSTANDING
OF ANYTHING OTHER THAN THEIR OWN
SELFISH NEEDS AND DESIRES...

A PEACE OF MIND ALWAYS SAYS YES, WHILE A FLUSTERED MIND FILLED WITH CONFUSSION USUALLY SAYS NO, OFTEN TIMES YOUR INDECISIVENESS BECOMES CLEARER WHEN THE MIND IS AT A POINT OF COMFORT...

SOMETIMES THE BEST EXPLANATION THAT U CAN GIVE IS NO EXPLANATION AT ALL BECAUSE TOSOME PEOPLE YOUR SILENCE CAN BE HEARD MUCH LOUDER AND CLEARER THAN YOUR WORDS WILL EVER BE...

A "STAND UP" GUY IS ALWAYS ACCOUNTABLE
FOR HIS MISTAKES AND ACTIONS EVEN
AMOUNGST HIS OWN EXSCUSES...

STOP WASTING YOUR TIME AND BLOCKING YOUR BLESSINGS BY CONTINUING TO DEAL WITH SO-CALLED "COMPLICATED SITUATIONS." HOW IS ANY SITUATION "COMPLICATED" THAT U HAVE NO DIRECT CONCRETE OBLIGATIONS TO? YOU ARE NOT A TREE, UPROOT AND KEEP IT MOVING...

NEVER FORGET, NEVER STOP, NEVER STEP
BACK, UNLESS ITS TO GAIN SUPPORT FOR YOUR
NEXT FEW STEPS FORWARD. ALSO, NEVER
LOOK BACK UNLESS ITS FOR A REFERENCE
POINT. FOR THE LIFE YOU LOOK TO OBTAIN IS
AHEAD OF YOU...

BE VERY CONSCIOUS OF YOUR JOURNEY THROUGH LIFE
SO THAT YOU MAY BE ABLE TO REFLECT ON WHERE
YOUR BLESSINGS STEMMED FROM. KNOWING THAT
EVERYTHING THAT HAPPENED TO YOU HAD TO HAPPEN
IN ORDER TO GET YOU TO WHERE YOU ARE...

BEFORE YOU PASS JUDGEMENT ON ANYONE
YOU HAVE TO ACKNOWLEDGE THAT LIFE ISNT
ALWAYS EASY. ACCEPT FULL RESPONSIBILITY
FOR ALL THE WRONG THAT YOU'VE DONE AND
APOLOGIZE FOR BEING HUMAN, KNOWING
THAT AT LEAST YOU HAVE A CONSCIENCE...

PEOPLE WILL PREACH A CERTAIN LEVEL OF
LOYALTY TO THE SAME PEOPLE THAT THEY
THEMSELVES FAIL TO SHOW THE SAME LEVEL
OF LOYALTY THAT THEY PLEDGE THEIR
ALLEGANCE TO...

IT'S A FUCKED UP REALITY BUT, IN MOST SITUATIONS, YOU WILL RECEIVE MORE HELP AND SUPPORT FROM YOUR FANS THAN YOU WILL YOUR OWN FRIENDS AND FAMILY... THINK ABOUT IT...

EVERY BLESSING IS ATTACHED TO A LESSON
JUST AS SOME GIFTS ARE ATTACHED WITH A
CURSE...

YOU CAN ALWAYS RUN OUT OF MONEY BUT AS LONG AS YOU DON'T EVER RUN OUT OF HUSTLE, YOU WILL ALWAYS HAVE THE WILL TO FIND A WAY...

WRITE DOWN YOUR DREAMS SO THAT THEY BECOME GOALS, BREAK DOWN YOUR GOALS SO THAT THEY BECOME A PLAN, INITIATE THE ACTION OF FOLLOWING THOSE STEPS WITHIN THE PLAN OF YOUR GOAL AND YOUR DREAMS WILL COME TRUE...

FORGET WHAT YOU WANT AND REMEMBER
WHAT YOU DESERVE... MOST PEOPLE
COMPLAIN ABOUT WANTING MORE, BUT
OFTEN TIMES THEY SET THEMSELVES UP IN
SITUATIONS WHERE THEY END UP SETTLING
FOR LESS...

OFTEN TIMES THE PEOPLE IN YOUR LIFE ARE
ONLY COMPATIBLE TO YOUR CURRENT SEASON
BECAUSE THEY CAN RELATE TO YOUR PAST OR
YOUR PRESENT BUT NOT YOUR FUTURE OR
YOUR NEXT SEASON...

PEOPLE PUT TOO MUCH EMPHASIS ON BEING IN A RELATIOINSHIP VS PUTTING THEIR PRIORITIES AND FOCUS ON WHAT THEY WANT AND NEED FOR THEMSELVES. THEREFORE, GIVING THEIR OBLIGATIONS TO THAT OTHER PERSON MORE SENIORITY OVER THEIR OWN PERSONAL PRIORITIES, PROGRESS, AND WELL BEING...

MORE OFTEN THAN NOT THE VALUE OF YOUR FRIENDSHIPS WILL QUICKLY BE DETERMINED BY THE AMOUNT OF MONEY THEY OWE YOU AND HOW, WHEN, OR WHETHER OR NOT THEY CHOOSE TO PAY YOU BACK...

IF YOU ARE HONEST WITH YOURSELF, IN LIFE THERE ARE NO RESET BUTTONS AND RARELY DO YOU GET A SECOND CHANCE AT DOING ANYTHING YOU FAILED AT DOING OR DIDN'T TAKE ADVANTAGE OF THE FIRST TIME. YOU ONLY GET ONE LIFE TO LIVE AND ONE CHANCE TO LIVE IT.

CARPE DIEM!

IF THEY DON'T CREATE HAPPINESS IN YOUR
LIFE, THEN DON'T ALLOW THEM THE POWER TO
TAKE IT AWAY...

BEWARE THE COMPANY THAT YOU KEEP FOR
EVERYONE ISN'T HAPPY FOR YOU NOR DO THEY
WANT TO SEE YOU HAPPY...

STOP ALLOWING PEOPLE TO INFLUENCE YOUR
MOOD AND FEEL SORRY FOR THOSE WHO PREY
ON YOU BECAUSE THEY HAVE YET TO FIND
THEIR OWN WAY...

LIFE IS GOING TO BE JUST THAT... LIFE... THE UPS THE DOWNS THE WINS THE LOSSES. BUT THE STRENGTH OF ENDURANCE WILL OFTEN SHOW YOUR PERSERVERANCE...

STOP DEALING WITH PEOPLE WHO CAN FIND TIME TO CATCH A FLIGHT BUT NOT TIME TO SEE YOU MINUTES AWAY IN THEIR OWN CITY. NOBODY IS BUSIER THAN A PERSON THAT'S NOT INTERESTED IN YOU. THEY REALLY AREN'T "THAT BUSY" THEY JUST AREN'T LEGITIMATELY INTERESTED...

THE TRUTH WILL NEVER TRULY SET YOU FREE IF
YOU ARE ALLOWING THE LIES TO HOLD YOU
HOSTAGE...

ENERGY IS HONEST....
MAKE THE BEST OF EVERY SITUATION BY
ALLOWING IT TO BE EXACTLY WHAT IT IS WITH
NO PRESSURE FROM THE IDEA OF WHAT YOU
THINK IT SHOULD BE. AND I KNOW IT SOUNDS
CRAZY BUT SOMETIMES THE MORE SERIOUS
PEOPLE "CLAIM" THAT THEY ARE, THE MORE
INDIRECT GAMES THEY TEND TO PLAY...
BUT THAT ENERGY...
IT NEVER LIES...

FIRST & FOREMOST I GIVE ALL PRAISE TO THE MOST HIGH FOR SHOWING ME GRACE. I WOULD ALSO LIKE TO THANK EVERY ONE OF YOU FOR YOUR SUPPORT! THANK YOU TO EVERYONE WHO PLAYED A PART IN HELPING ME TO BRING THIS PROJECT INTO FRUITION. WHETHER IT WAS HANDS ON, THE PASSING OF INFORMATION, OR JUST KEEPING ME MOTIVATED & PUSHING ME TO GET IT DONE, I TRULY APPRECIATE YOU ALL! IT'S BEEN YEARS IN THE MAKING & A PLETHORA OF OBSTACLES INCLUDING MY 3YR CUSTODY CASE. (BOOK COMING SOON) BUT WE FINALLY MADE! WE DID IT! WE ARE ON OUR WAY!

A DEDICATION TO MY MOTIVATION...

I WOULD LIKE TO DEDICATE THIS SERIES TO MY MOM WHO HAS AND ALWAYS WILL BE THERE IN MY CORNER HANDS DOWN! I LOVE YOU MOM! AND TO MY SON MR. MASON... EVERYTHING IN ME I GIVE TO YOU... AND LAST BUT NOT LEAST I'D LIKE TO GIVE A SPECIAL SHOUTOUT TO ALL OF THOSE LOST IN THE STRUGGLE, TO ALL OF THOSE WE HAVE LOST ALONG OUR WAY IN THIS THING CALLED LIFE... MAY WE CELEBRATE ALL OF THEIR LIVES RATHER THAN MOURNING THEIR LOSSES...

Made in the USA
Columbia, SC
31 January 2025

53058821R00059